FREE Coloring Pages!

Receive your FREE coloring pages directly to your email!

1.Scan the QR Code below!
2. Open the link
3. Enter your email address

DURAND
BOOKS

Visit Durandbooks.com

Written by Durand Loy
Illustrations by Katerina Rusakova

Published by Durand Books
Visit www.durandbooks.com

THE CHRISTIAN COLORING BOOK FOR KIDS

By Durand Loy

Illustrated By Katerina Rusakova

DURAND BOOKS

This book belongs to:

_____

Creation

In the beginning, God created light, land, and creatures. On the sixth day, He sculpted humans, Adam and Eve, in His image, placing them in the beautiful Garden of Eden. This revelation reveals the magnificent story of God's creative power and love for His creation.

Garden of Eden

God created the first man called Adam and the first woman
called Eve. He placed them in the Garden of Eden.
Adam and Eve lived in paradise until they disobeyed God,
leading to their expulsion.

NOAH'S ARK

The story of Noah and the Ark is about a man chosen by God to build an ark and save pairs of animals from a great flood.

Joseph and His Coat

Joseph, the favored son, received a coat of many colors from his father, sparking jealousy among his brothers.
Joseph was betrayed and sold into slavery, which lead to a tale of resilience, forgiveness, and God's ultimate plan.

Moses and the Burning Bush

God appeared to Moses in a burning bush, instructing him to
lead the Israelites out of slavery in Egypt. After Moses'
encounter with the burning bush he played an important role
in delivering his people.

Red Sea crossing

God parted the Red Sea to help the Israelites, led by Moses,
escape from Egyptian forces.
The sea closed back, saving the Israelites.

The Ten Commandments

On Mount Sinai, God gave Moses the Ten Commandments, a set of moral and ethical principles to guide the Israelites. These commandments form the foundation of Judeo-Christian ethics.

The Battle of Jericho

Joshua led the Israelites around Jericho's walls, and with a mighty shout, the walls crumbled, showcasing God's miraculous power and the victory of faith over seemingly impossible challenges.

Samson pushing down columns

God gave Samson great strength; he pushed down the pillars of a Philistine temple, sacrificing himself to defeat his enemies.

David and Goliath

A young brave shepherd named David faced the giant warrior
Goliath with just a sling and a stone.
With faith in God, David defeated Goliath, because his
strength came from trust in the Almighty.

Daniel in the Lion's Den

Daniel was thrown into a den of lions because of his strong faith. God protected Daniel, and he left the den unharmed, demonstrating the power of faith and divine intervention.

Jonah and the Whale

Jonah, disobeying God's command, tried to escape but was swallowed by a great fish. After three days and nights in the belly of the fish, Jonah repented, and God commanded the fish to release him.

The Birth of Jesus

In Bethlehem, Mary gave birth to Jesus, the Son of God, in a humble manger. Angels proclaimed the news to shepherds, and wise men followed a star to bring gifts to the newborn King.

Three Wise Men

Wise men from the East followed a star to find the newborn
Jesus, presenting gifts of gold, frankincense, and myrrh,
acknowledging him as the prophesied King.

Jesus feeds 5000 people

Jesus miraculously multiplied a small amount of fish and bread to feed a multitude of five thousand, showcasing his compassion and divine power.

Jesus walks on water

Jesus displayed his divinity by walking on the Sea of Galilee during a storm. At Jesus' invitation, Peter briefly walked on water but began to sink when he doubted.

The Mustard Seed

Jesus compared the Kingdom of Heaven to a tiny mustard seed that grows into a mighty tree, illustrating the incredible impact of even the most minor acts of faith and love when nurtured by God's grace.

The Healing of the Blind Bartimaeus

Blind Bartimaeus, hearing of Jesus, cried out for mercy. Jesus restored his sight, commending his faith, showing Christ's compassion and the transformative power of faith.

Jesus Calming the Storm

Caught in a storm-tossed sea, Jesus calmed the waves with a simple command, demonstrating His authority over nature and inspiring faith by showing that even the fiercest storms bow to His power.

The Good Samaritan

Jesus told a parable about a compassionate Samaritan who helped a wounded man on the road, highlighting the importance of love and mercy towards others.

The Parable of the Lost Sheep

Jesus shared the story of a shepherd joyfully rescuing one lost sheep, emphasizing God's boundless love and the profound rejoicing in heaven over one repentant soul.

The Prodigal Son

Jesus told a story about a wayward son who spent his inheritance. His father welcomed him back with open arms. This story illustrates God's unconditional love and forgiveness for those who repent.

Palm Sunday

As Jesus entered Jerusalem on a donkey, crowds welcomed Him with palm branches, recognizing Him as the promised Messiah. The joyous occasion marked the beginning of the events leading to Jesus' crucifixion and resurrection.

Last Supper

Jesus shared a final meal with his disciples before his crucifixion.
During the meal, he showed the sacrament of communion, symbolizing his body and blood.

The Resurrection of Jesus

After Jesus was crucified and buried he rose from the dead on the third day, conquering sin and death. His resurrection is central to the Christian faith, signifying redemption and eternal life.

Paul's Shipwreck

Facing a strong storm, Paul reassured the crew of God's plan, and despite a shipwreck, all on board safely reached an island, highlighting God's providence and Paul's unwavering faith.

Armor of God

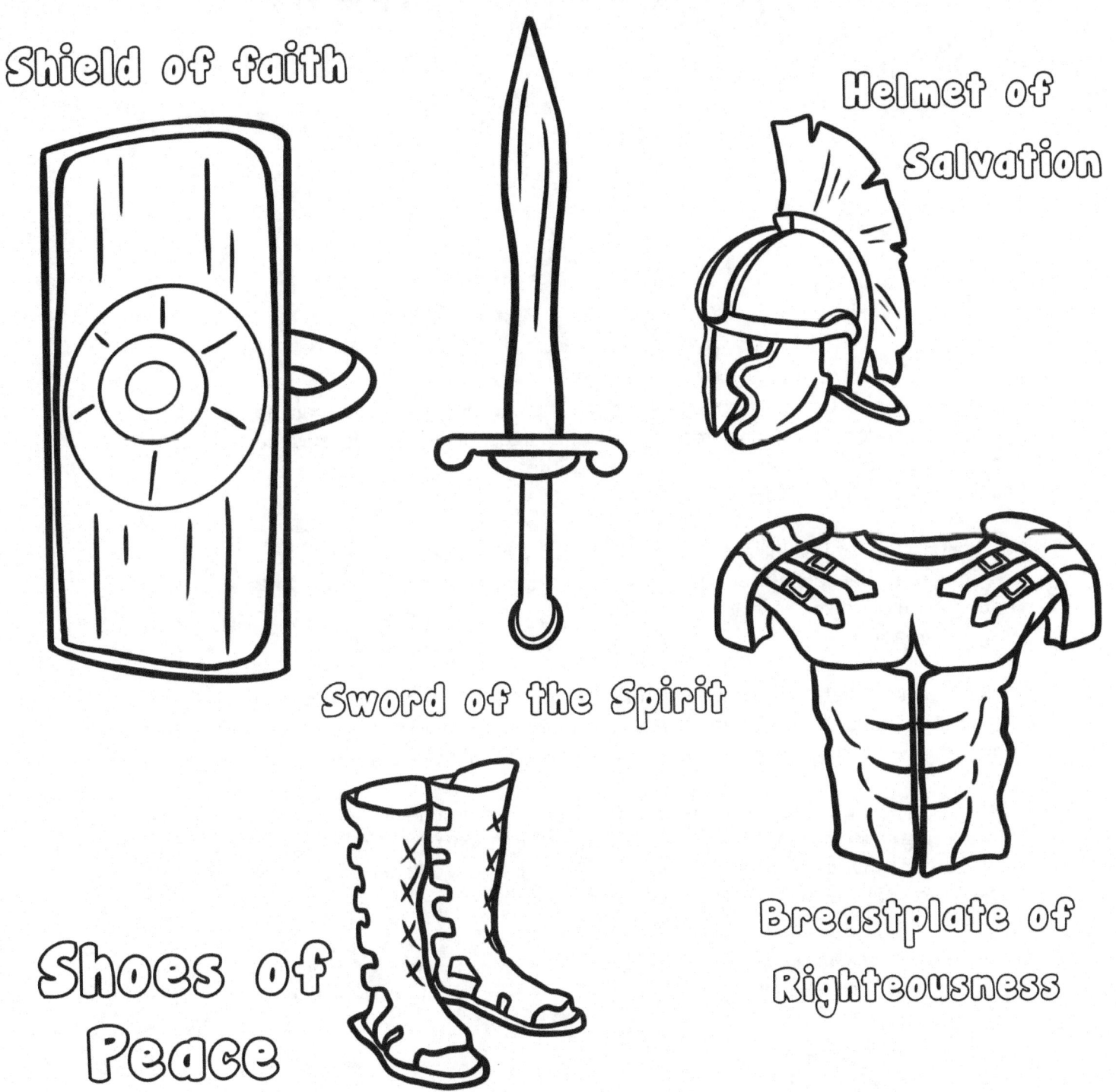

Shield of faith

Helmet of Salvation

Sword of the Spirit

Breastplate of Righteousness

Shoes of Peace

Paul encouraged believers to wear the invisible Armor of God, protecting them in life's battles with truth, righteousness, peace, faith, salvation, and the Word of God, empowering them to stand firm in faith and trust in God's strength.

About the Author

Durand Loy, a native of Natchez, Mississippi, is an author deeply committed to crafting enriching literary experiences for children of all ages. Born and raised in the heart of the South, Durand draws inspiration from his Southern roots and family life as a devoted husband and father of two young boys.

With a passion for instilling strong moral and ethical values in children, Durand specializes in creating faith-based children's books and engaging coloring books. His works are not only educational but also serve as tools for fostering character development and spiritual growth in young readers.

Driven by his belief in the power of storytelling, Durand endeavors to make learning and reading enjoyable experiences for children. Through his books, he seeks to spark curiosity, encourage empathy, and promote understanding, all while imparting valuable life lessons.

Durand Loy's dedication to creating uplifting and wholesome literature reflects his unwavering commitment to nurturing the minds and hearts of the next generation. With each page turn, he invites readers on a journey of imagination, discovery, and, above all, the celebration of love, faith, and family values.

Scan the QR code below to follow me on Facebook!

Scan the QR code below to visit us at Durandbooks.com

A Note From the Author

Dear Readers,

I'm writing to express my gratitude for your support and to kindly request a small favor.

Reviews on platforms like Amazon play a crucial role in helping potential readers discover new books. Your honest opinion could be the deciding factor for someone on the fence about picking up one of my books.

If you find these coloring pages to be engaging and fun, please consider taking a moment to share your thoughts on Amazon. Your review doesn't need to be lengthy; even a few words about what resonated with you would be immensely valuable.

Your feedback not only helps other readers but also provides me with invaluable insight into what aspects of my publications are working well and where there may be room for improvement.

Thank you for considering my request, and thank you once again for your support of my work. Your support means the world to me.

Please scan the QR code below to find all of my books in one place on Amazon.com.

Warm regards,
Durand

Check out our other popular Christian children's books!

Scan the QR Code below

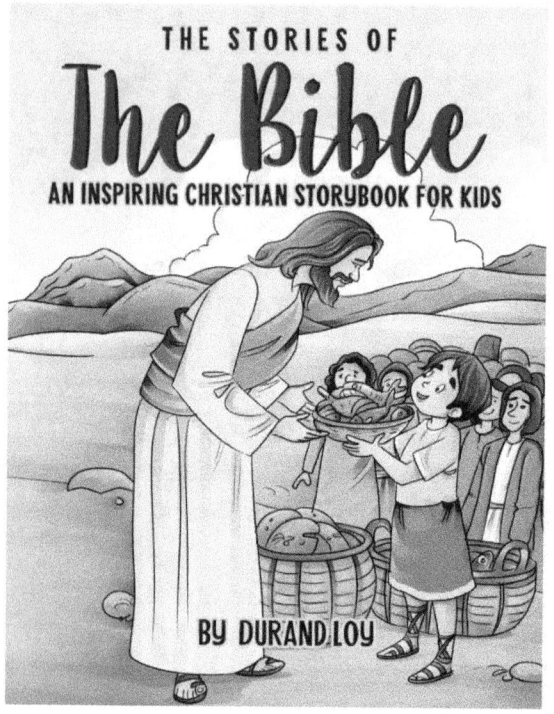

The Stories of The Bible
By Durand Loy

Color The Stories of The Bible
By Durand Loy